Dadsongs
Remembering a Loved One's Melody

BY TIA BARBERO ILLUSTRATED BY PAUL BARBERO

Ferne Press

Dadsongs
Copyright © 2010 by Tia Barbero
Illustrated by Paul Barbero
Layout and cover design by Raphael Giuffrida and Kimberly Franzen
Printed in Canada

Summary: The story of a seven-year-old girl dealing with the cancer diagnosis and death of her father as she realizes that, even after someone dies, traditions and memories remain.

Illustrations created with acrylic paint, colored pencil, and graphite.

Library of Congress Cataloging-in-Publication Data
    Barbero, Tia
    Dadsongs: Remembering a Loved One's Melody / Tia Barbero – First Edition
    ISBN-13: 978-1-933916-50-7
      1. Death of a parent. 2. Juvenile Fiction.
    I. Barbero, Tia II. Dadsongs: Remembering a Loved One's Melody
    Library of Congress Control Number: 2009939677

Dedicated to all the family and friends who helped us heal through listening, laughing, and loving arms.

FERNE PRESS

Ferne Press is an imprint of Nelson Publishing & Marketing
366 Welch Road, Northville, MI 48167
www.nelsonpublishingandmarketing.com
(248) 735-0418

"What's going to happen to Daddy?" I asked my sister, Francie, after Mom and Dad told us about the cancer inside of him, and that's the biggest question racing through my brain.

"Mary, you heard them," said Paul, my big brother. "Don't worry, because we're going to fight this cancer."
How can we do that? I wondered.

"Mom and Dad already made doctor appointments, and we can't give up hope. We have to pull together and help each other," Francie told me.

My daddy is so smart and funny. He bursts through the door every night greeting us with a big "Hey, hey, hey!" a hug for me, a kiss for Mom, and a pat for the kitty.

He loves to play his guitar and teaches us all about music. So much music! There isn't a day without Daddy making music.

No matter where we go—church, camping with the neighbors, sitting in the backyard, or on the front porch—Daddy plays his guitar. If it were alive, it would be his best friend.

He likes to dance, too. He'll sneak up on Mom while she's doing the dishes and swing her around to the tunes coming from the radio. I giggle, Paul thinks it's gross, and Francie just smiles and sings along.

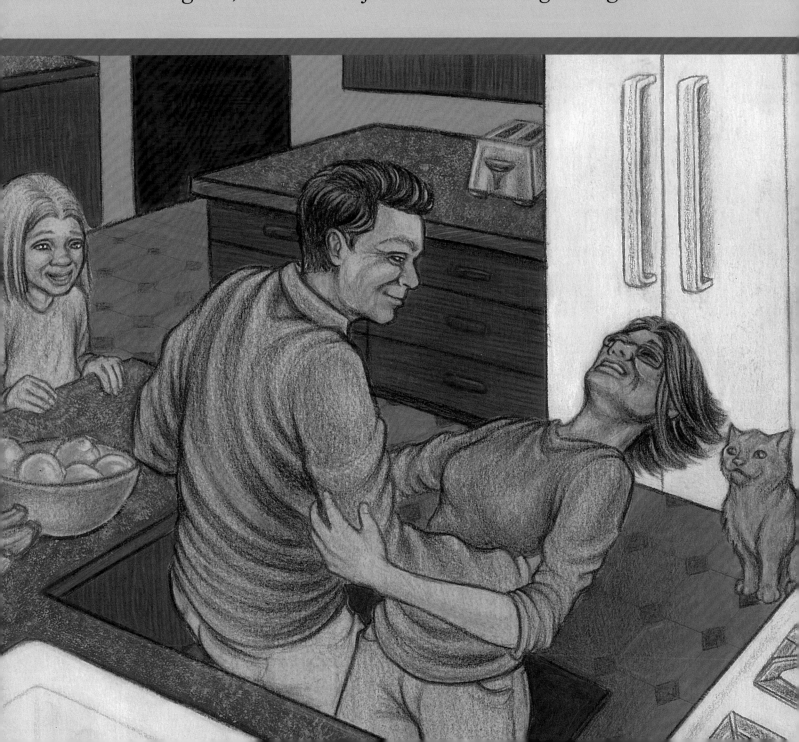

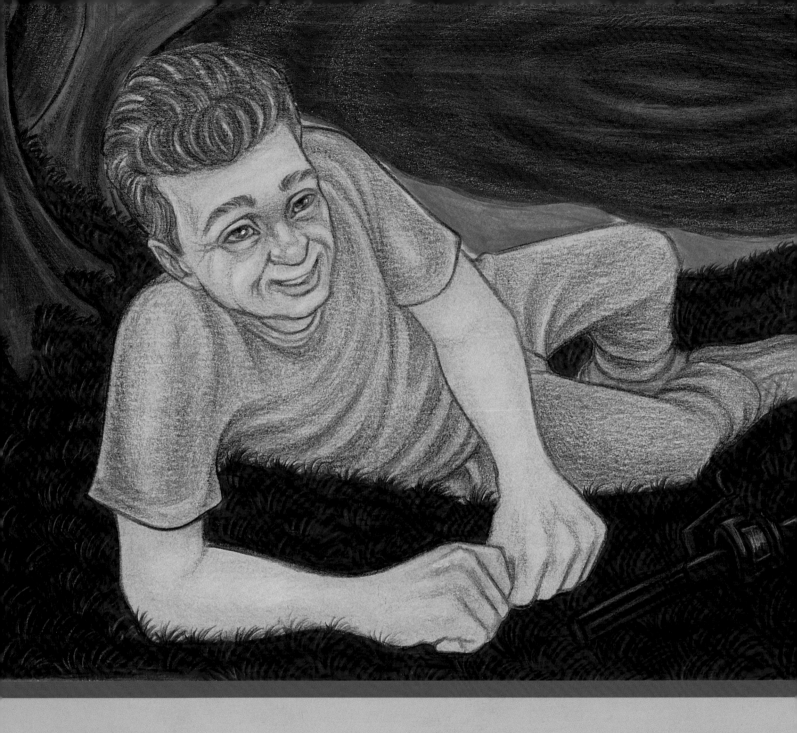

I love to hang out with Daddy. We go bird watching early on summer mornings, and he teaches me about the songs of the birds. He baits my hook when we go fishing, 'cause I don't like to kill the worms.

And he's not too grown up to catch lightning bugs after supper. On August nights, we lie down in the backyard waiting for shooting stars.

"Oh, Daddy, please don't die!"

Life is changing pretty quickly. Francie and Mom take turns driving Daddy to the hospital for his treatments. Paul mows the lawn without complaining.

Daddy's friends come over and do chores that he planned to do but doesn't have the strength for. The moms in the neighborhood make us dinners. Everybody is helping us.

I'm only seven. What can I do?

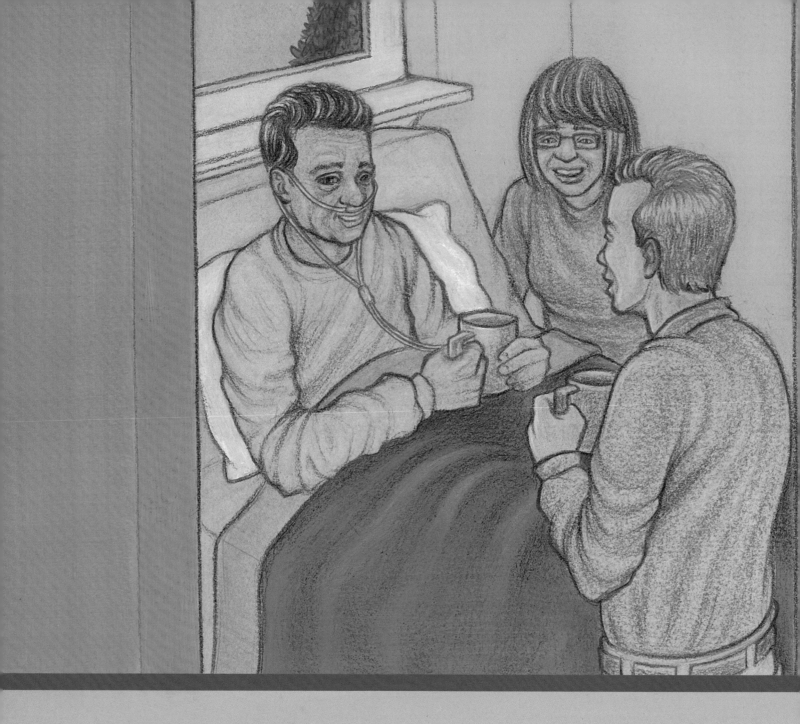

Every day Daddy gets weaker, so they put a hospital bed in the living room and we make space for medical stuff. The noise of the oxygen machine is so scary. It sounds like a monster.

Aunts and uncles and friends stop by. So many visitors. I watch Daddy smile at each one. I wish they would all go away. Are they here to cheer him up, or are they saying goodbye?

The coolest thing about this is that Daddy is home. Now I can spend as much time as I want with him.

"Mary, you give the best foot rubs in the whole world."

I'll give him a million foot rubs while I sit on his bed and we share stories.

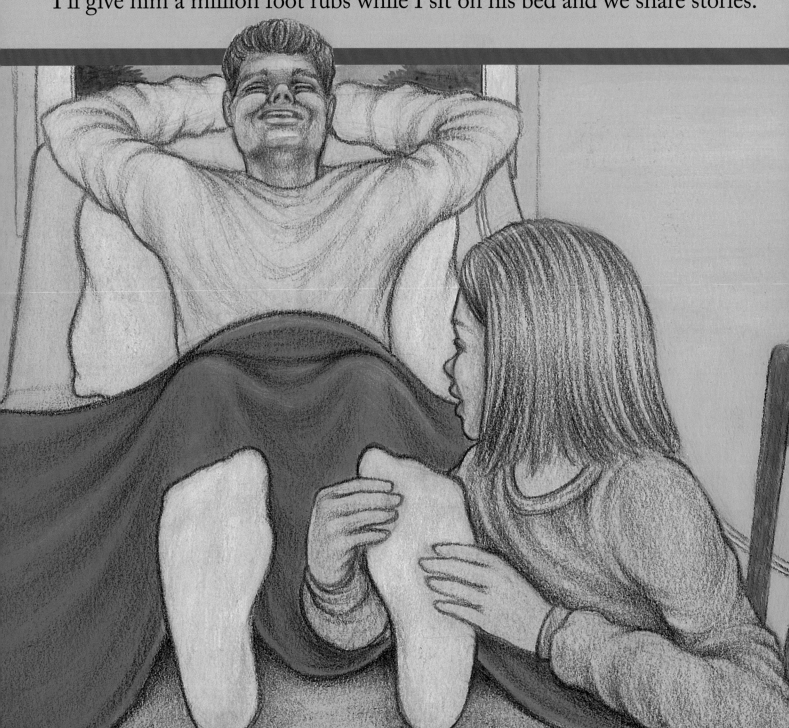

We listen to the songs on the boom box that remind him of me and Francie and Paul—lullabies, funny tunes, and driving songs. There are about a hundred songs that remind him of Mom. He tells me tales about each one. We make a list of them while I brush his hair.

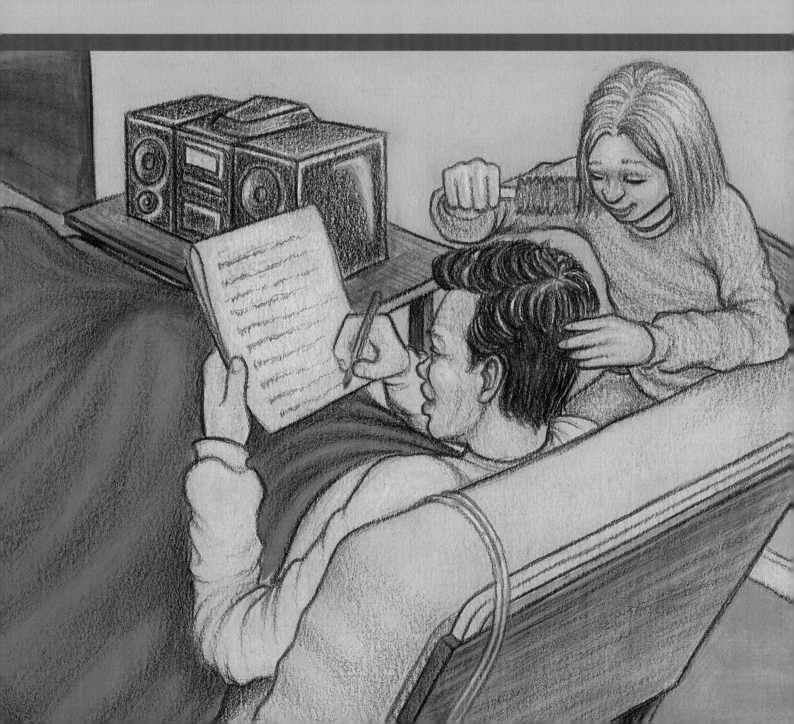

"Daddy, I'm scared. Are you afraid?"
"It will be different, but we'll always be a family. I'm not afraid of heaven.
I'm afraid to leave all of you. But I believe that somehow, darlin', I will
always be near."
"Even from heaven?" I ask.
"Heaven for me is being with you."

Every day the cancer changes Daddy's body. He's tired during the day and awake at night. Someone stays with him all the time. We sit with him talking, listening, or in silence. It's hard to look at him because he isn't strong anymore. But he can still hold my hand.

Then one night as we sat and prayed with him, he said "I love you" and fell asleep. That's when he left for heaven.

"Oh, Daddy, can I come with you?"

The next few days are a whirlwind. People coming and going. Hugs from strangers. Brave smiles from aunts and uncles. Then the funeral and the burial. I cry until I run out of tears. "Goodbye, my Daddy."

We stay close to home and to each other for the rest of the summer. Francie and I run around catching lightning bugs. It feels good to think of bugs.

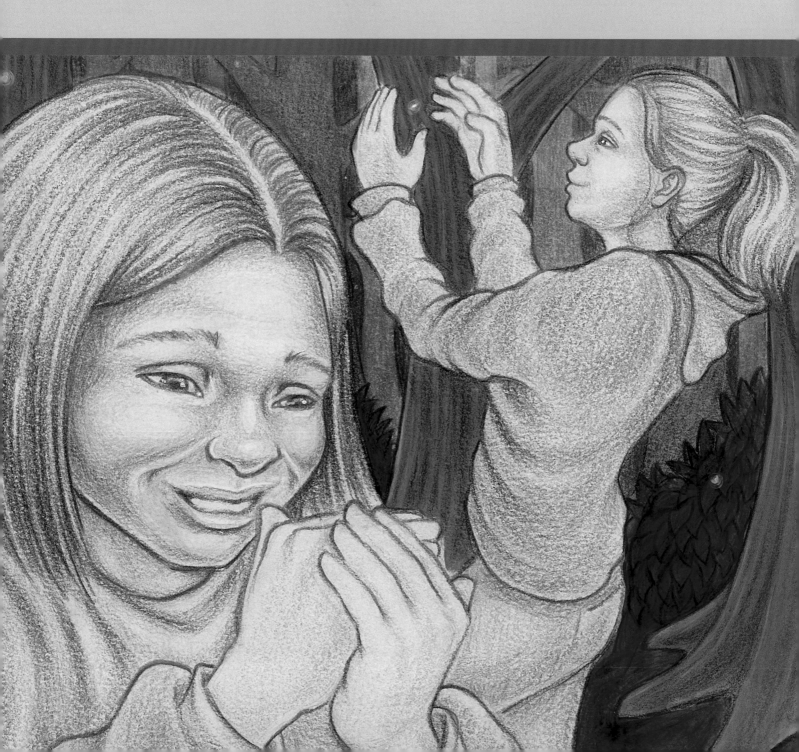

Right before school begins, Paul and I walk to the pond in the park and he puts a worm on my hook. It's good to think about worms and fish.

I tell Francie and Paul about the list of songs that Daddy made, and they have a great idea.
"Can we put Daddy's special songs on the computer and talk about Daddy?" I ask Francie and Paul. It takes a long time, but by winter we've made our own playlist called "Dadsongs."

As we lie on the floor with our eyes closed, listening to the music, pictures of Daddy flash through my memory. It's like a movie inside of me. I see his smile, hear his "Hey, hey, hey!", and watch him singing in the kitchen.

His songs are like soft rain on me. The melodies whirl me and surround me like a gentle warm hug. Yes, our family has changed and I miss him so much, but Daddy is always near whenever there is music.

Dear Reader:

While I do not claim to be an expert on grief and healing, I've been there after losing our daughter and my husband, and I can only share what has helped us. My husband, Chris, was a gentle man who loved music. At first, it hurt to listen to his special songs. But in time, his tunes became a comforting way of remembering him and his love for us. We talk about him every day, not forced but in a natural way: "Remember when Dad used to…" or "Dad would really love this." In this way, he is still a part of our lives.

If your loved one was a garden fanatic, go play in the dirt and talk as if they are right there with you. You will probably be inspired. If they were finicky housekeepers, go clean out the fridge. The sparkle will be a reminder of them. If they had the gift of hospitality, throw a dinner party and talk about the funny times you had together. Remember.

You cannot have enough laughter in your life. Don't be afraid of joy. It will start slowly if you allow yourself to accept joy when it presents itself—a baby's smile, a dog's shenanigans, a funny movie, a card game with friends. Don't stifle your smiles, because the one you miss does not desire your unhappiness and I believe that they are closer than we think. I asked Chris before he died to send me a rainbow so I knew everything was going to be all right. I have run into a rainbow every day since his passing. Love never dies.

Remember too, that it's okay to cry, feel angry, or be confused. That's all part of healing. If you feel that the people around you are uncomfortable talking about your loved one, find someone else who loved them and who will listen to you. And let the little ones in your life grieve in their own time and in their own way. Hug and enjoy them. Be proud of them. They are a gift to you. Be a gift to them.

Tia Barbero

About the Author

Tia Barbero was born in Philadelphia, the oldest of thirteen children, and learned to laugh and change diapers at a very early age. She has either been a kid or around kids her whole life. It is easy for her to remember the feelings she felt when she was little, and she cherishes the memories of childhood. Working with students from preschool through high school, there hasn't been a kid she couldn't love. Tia loves art and will do anything to instill art literacy in every child who will listen. A volunteer for many years at the Plymouth Community Arts Council, she developed a storytelling program that teaches kids about art. She resides with three of her children in Canton, Michigan. For more information, please visit her at www.tiabarberobooks.com.

About the Illustrator

Paul Barbero studied fine art at Siena Heights University and Tyler School of Art, where his professors encouraged him to develop his natural talent for illustration. Illustrations for his first book, *Dadsongs*, were inspired by his own memories. In addition to illustrating, Paul's interests include flame working, painting, and music.